Hello!
I am a turtle.

I0115148

Turtles that live in the water usually live longer than turtles that live on land.

A turtle's shell is made of bone, "cartilage", and "keratin".

Your ears and nose are made of cartilage.

Your hair and nails are made of keratin.

The shell of a turtle is made up of over 50 bones and is part of their skeleton.

Could you please stop touching my skeleton?

Unlike tortoises, turtles can't retract their heads and limbs into their shells.

Some turtles are "herbivores".

That means I only eat plants, not animals.

Some turtles are "ominvores".

That means I eat both plants and animals.

Some snapping turtles have a unique lure on their tongues to attract prey.

Just come a little closer.

It's a snap!

Snapping turtles have powerful jaws and can crush hard-shelled prey.

A turtle's flippers helps them speed through the water.

Some of us can reach speeds of up to 22 miles per hour (35 km/h).

The sleek shape of the turtle's shell lets them swim faster in the water.

Sea turtles can hold their breath for several hours.

My body is specially made, so I can stay down here a long time.

Turtles can store oxygen in their muscles and tissues.

Some turtles species often bask together on logs or rocks near the water's edge.

Basking helps us regulate our body temperature.

Basking in groups helps turtles to keep watch for predators together.

Some turtles gather in groups. Others prefer to be alone.

Turtles sometimes become aggressive to compete for basking sites.

They might head bob, hiss, push, shove, or bite.

Turtles communicate through body language.

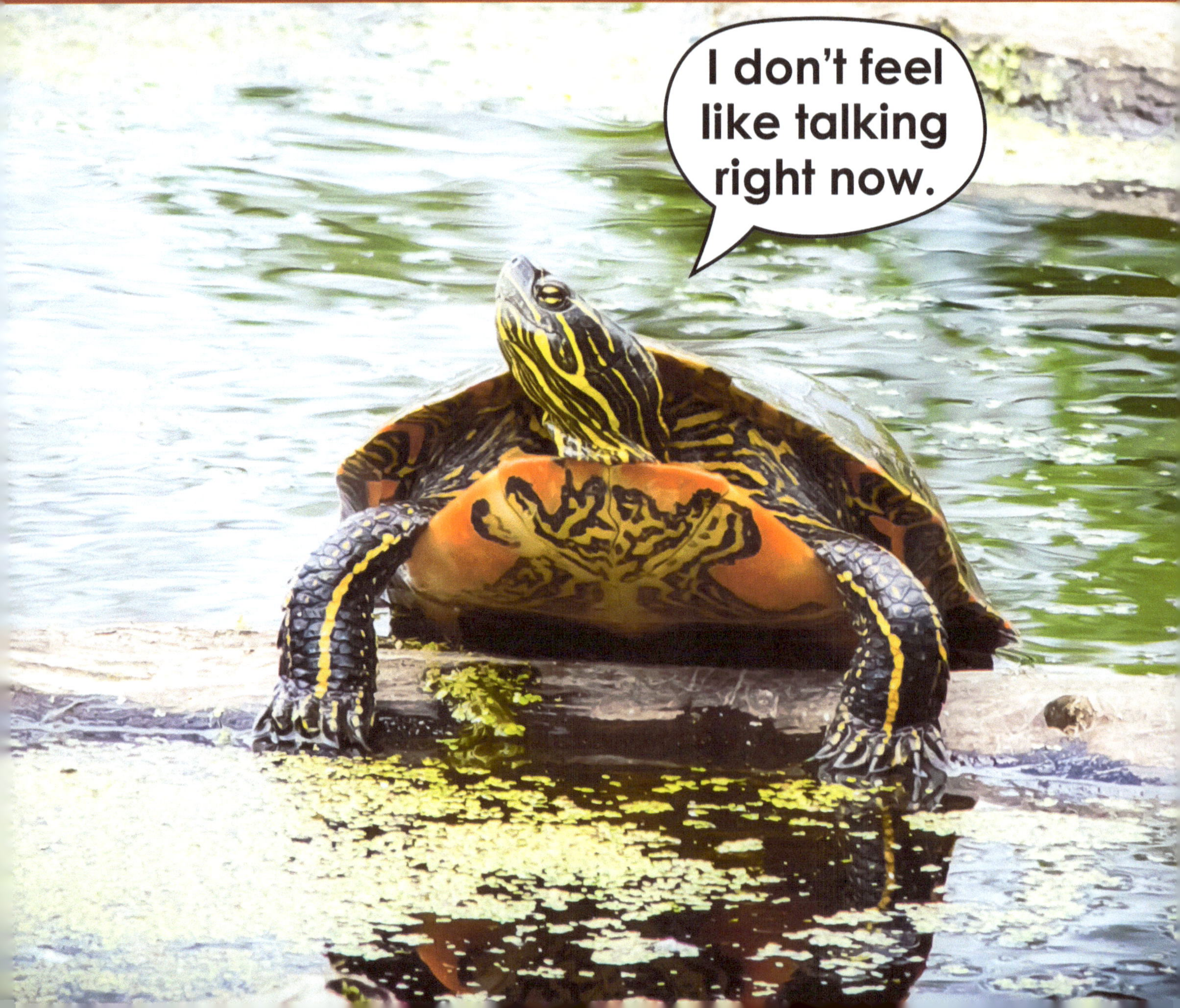

Would you like to go for a swim later?

Male turtles may bob their heads or swim around a female when looking for a mate.

Turtles have a strong sense of smell.

My nose helps me find food.

Most turtles lay their eggs in nests that they dig in the sand or soil.

This looks like a nice place.

The heat from the sun helps keep the eggs warm and helps them develop.

When turtles are born, we are called "hatchlings".

Hatchlings are usually on their own right from the moment they hatch.

I have to find food, avoid predators, and navigate the ocean all by myself.

Once sea turtle hatchlings leave the nest, they head straight for the ocean.

Ready for adventure!

Other types of turtle hatchings stay near the nest after hatching.

I'll keep safe here for a while.

Turtles use the Earth's magnetic field.

I know where I'm going.

It helps them find their way home after a long trip.

Some turtles travel thousands of miles for foraging and nesting.

Want more?

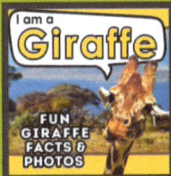      

 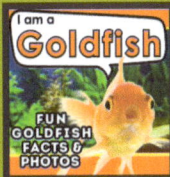     

  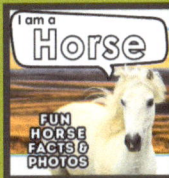    

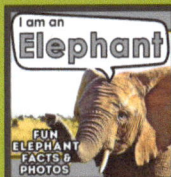 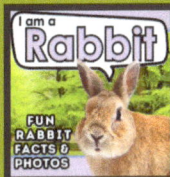    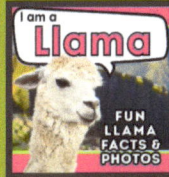 

     ... and more

COLLECT THEM ALL!

ActiveBrainsBooks.com

Hello parents!

Visit us to find out about new releases and **FREE** offers. We'll let you know when we have a new release coming out and how you can get it for FREE.

And you can cast your vote for what book we make next!

scan here

or visit here

ActiveBrainsBooks.com

---

scan here

Let us know what you think. As an independent publisher, your honest reviews mean a lot to us and our business. We'd love to hear from you!

amazon.com/review/create-review/

or visit here

FOLLOW US on Amazon.

amazon.com/author/activebrainsbooks

ActiveBrainsBooks.com

ACTIVE BRAINS

www.ingramcontent.com/pod-product-compliance
Lightning Source LLC
Chambersburg PA
CBHW060845270326
41933CB00003B/195